The Wonders
of Solitude

The Wonders of Solitude

Selected and with
an Introduction
by
DALE SALWAK

THE CLASSIC WISDOM COLLECTION
NEW WORLD LIBRARY
SAN RAFAEL, CALIFORNIA

The Classic Wisdom Collection
Published by New World Library
58 Paul Drive, San Rafael, CA 94903

Cover design: Greg Wittrock
Cover photo: Carr Clifton
Text design: Nancy Benedict
Typography: Stephanie Eichleay

Library of Congress Cataloging-in-Publication Data

The wonders of solitude / edited by Dale Salwak.
    p. cm. — (The classic wisdom collection)
ISBN 1-880032-53-8 : $12.95
1. Solitude — Quotations, maxims, etc.
I. Salwak, Dale. II. Series.
BJ1499.S6W66   1995
128'.4 — dc20   94-40474
                                         CIP

ISBN 1-880032-53-8
Printed in the U.S.A. on acid-free paper
Distributed by Publishers Group West
10 9 8 7 6 5 4 3 2 1

For Jim and Heather Shuemaker

Contents

Publisher's Preface

Life is an endless cycle of change. We and our world will never remain the same.

Every generation has difficulty relating to the previous generation; even the language changes. The child speaks a different language than the parent.

It seems almost miraculous, then, that certain voices, certain books, are able to speak not only to one, but to many generations beyond them. The plays and poems of William Shakespeare are still relevant today — still capable of giving us goose bumps, still entertaining, disturbing, and profound. Shakespeare is the writer who, in the English language, defines the word *classic*.

There are many other writers and thinkers who, for a great many reasons, can be considered classic, for they withstand the test of time. We want to present the best of them to you in the New World Library Classic Wisdom Collection. Even though these writers and thinkers may have lived many years ago, they are still relevant and important in today's world for the enduring words of wisdom they created, words that should forever be kept in print.

The Wonders of Solitude is a very special book in this collection. It is, at various times, profound, enlightened, touching, poetic, and inspired. Every citizen of the planet Earth can gain value from the words and insights contained between these covers.

We hope it inspires you, as it has inspired us, to create more solitude in our lives, and to value that solitude more highly. It is only through silence that we can truly discover ourselves, our sources of creativity, and our unique contribution we all have to make to this beautiful world we all share.

Marc Allen
New World Library

Introduction

At one time or another all of us, I believe, hear the call to solitude. It can come upon us at any moment, under any circumstances — during times of good health or the trials of infirmity, after abandonment or the death of a loved one, in childhood or later in life, in crowds, voluntarily or imposed. Sometimes, it sneaks up on us, much like the persistent ache of a hunger that no sustenance from our fellow human beings can satisfy. Or it beckons as a still, quiet voice from within — the voice of God.

At such moments many of us feel a desire, as Henry David Thoreau did well over a century ago, to go to the woods to "live deliberately, to front only the essential facts of life," to remove ourselves from our peripheral concerns, from the pressures of a madly active world, and to return to the center where life is sacred — a humble miracle and mystery. Nothing could be worse, Thoreau wrote, than to come to the end of life and "discover that I had not lived."

As Thoreau suggests, in confronting "only the

essential facts of life" we meet ourselves face-to-face; and for many of us, that experience can be rewarding, often life-changing, raising us to the heights of ecstasy, self-awareness, and creativity. In solitude, we may find a new beginning, an opportunity to break old habits. In solitude, we may find increased sensitivity, compassion, and empathy. In solitude, we may find the truth of ourselves, restore our dulled senses, and clarify and reorder our priorities. Above all, in solitude, we may find God, and come to hear that voice.

Whether for reasons of preparation, study, creation, penitence, self-examination, reflection, purification or prayer — solitude is the most fundamental of all the spiritual disciplines, and we must return to it again and again if we hope to hear the soft voice of inspiration, if we want to live fully realized lives.

Like so many proponents of thoughtful solitude whom I include in this book, my own enthusiasm for it began in childhood. Although not necessarily a loner, even then I felt naturally inclined to spending long stretches of quiet time alone; I would take walks, read or listen to music, or just lie down and venture, I suppose, as deeply as I could into myself. I came to trust the small, quiet voice that speaks so eloquently on every decision in life, that helps us to find out what is best for ourselves and our own nature.

Fortunately, my brother and I had parents who understood, supported and even encouraged our inclinations; indeed, "quiet time apart" became as natural for us as perpetual noise and confusion seemed to be for our next-door neighbors. We welcomed our time together, but we also treasured our time apart, and our intimacy with and understanding one another grew richer as a result. I am grateful to my parents not only for creating the space that enabled me to pursue the joy of solitude, but also for teaching me that no journey is more exciting, more adventurous, and more revealing than the journey within.

Now, years later and married, I find I have an ever-growing need to make that journey, and what's more, my family has developed a similar inclination. My son, since turning five, has more than once said to me, "Daddy, I want to be alone for awhile," or "Can we have some quiet time?" And both my wife and I have learned to create weekly if not daily opportunities to step aside from our busy lives to inquire of their meaning and purpose. Far from being a waste of time, these periods are often exactly what we need to find the energy and inner peace to return to the world and transmit what we have learned.

This is not to say that solitude always requires our absence from people. Some of our most meaningful times with others have been spent in shared silence while walking along a beach, sitting on the steps, reading. With friends, relatives, even strangers — at home, at work, in houses of worship, in business, in marriage, on a crowded city street — we can still retire within ourselves and be immersed in solitude. Indeed, some people seek out crowds so that anonymity can help them feel alone.

And yet, in a secular world that devalues those who make time to listen to themselves, in a society that tends to equate a need for solitude with laziness, inactivity, and nonproductiveness, I suspect that many people have lost possession of what Emily Dickinson has called the "appetite for silence." In school and at home, among friends and at play, there seems to be ever-lessening opportunities for quiet time apart. And as people grow older and their lives become steadily more hectic and fragmented, they find themselves caught up in a race against time with no time for themselves.

How do we find solitude? Why is it so important to our lives? And how can we reconcile what most of us feel to be the daily tug-of-war between the spirit of community and the spirit of solitariness? To answer these questions, and others, over ten years ago I began to collect everything I could find buried in the writings of the variously solitary lives of a wide range of people — poets and novelists, playwrights, essayists and politicians, artists, explorers, philosophers, psychologists, physicians, theologians. Out of the resulting collection I have brought together the best and then clustered the material around several important themes that are the basis for the divisions in this book. For those who have the habit of solitude, and for those who do not, I hope that what follows will be a welcome companion for encouragement, comfort, and inspiration.

For their help when it was most needed, I am indebted to the following good people: Dr. Reginald Clarke, Peggy B. Harding, Manley Johnson, Laura Nagy, my parents Dr. Stanley and Frances H. Salwak, Mildred Sharpsteen, my brother Glenn, and my wife Patti, guardian of my solitude. I also owe a special debt of gratitude to my pastor and friend, Dr. Lloyd J. Ogilvie, who generously gave me the title for this book and from whose many afternoon discussions with me I have benefitted immeasurably.

Dale Salwak
Citrus College
Glendora, CA

1

A Noisy World

Nothing has changed the nature of man so much as the loss of silence. The invention of printing, technics, compulsory education — nothing has so altered man as this lack of relationship to silence, this fact that silence is no longer taken for granted, as something as natural as the sky above or the air we breathe. Man who has lost silence has not merely lost one human quality but his whole structure has been changed thereby.

MAX PICARD, FRENCH PHILOSOPHER

The Industrial Revolution brought with it gadgets to use up our time and to fill our world with sounds that not only drown out the voice of God, but also destroy the silence which is the proper environment for the nurturing of Man's soul. Think about your own life. Take just one day of the week. If your home is typical, you get up in the morning feeling harried and hurried. You must wash, dress, have breakfast, and, if you have children, get them ready for school. Somehow, in all this hurry and confusion, you turn on the radio or television to get the morning news. There doesn't seem to be enough confusion and chaos in the home, so you let in the world's share of confusion and chaos to add to that already existing, and in addition, raise the noise level. We seem, in our time, to be afraid of silence. For, if we get into our cars to go to work, we are apt to immediately turn on the radio instead of enjoying a time of relative quiet.

KARL PRUTER, AMERICAN BISHOP

Architects believe less and less in doors these days, so that houses are becoming like beehives, arches leading into chambers and more arches. It is lucky that Americans are still puritans in their habits. You can be alone in the bathroom.

SALLY WEINRAUB
AMERICAN SOCIAL CRITIC

Whenever we have a little free time, most of us seek some form of amusement. We pick up a serious book, a novel, or a magazine. If we are in America we turn on the radio or the television, or we indulge in incessant talk. There is a constant demand to be amused, to be entertained, to be taken away from ourselves. . . . Very few of us ever walk in the fields and the woods, not talking or singing songs, but just walking quietly and observing things about us and within ourselves.

J. KRISHNAMURTI, INDIAN PHILOSOPHER

If one sets aside time for a business engagement, a trip to the hairdresser, a social engagement, or a shopping expedition, that time is accepted as inviolable. But if one says: I cannot come because that is my hour to be alone, one is considered rude, egotistical or strange. What a commentary on our civilization, when being alone is considered suspect; when one has to apologize for it, make excuses, hide the fact that one practices it — like a secret vice!

ANNE MORROW LINDBERGH
AMERICAN AUTHOR

We are a people either unused to being alone or actually afraid of it. We have for so long talked and eaten, argued and thought, sung and even read in groups, that we are at a loss how to manage our minds or our bodies alone.

MARY ELLEN CHASE, AMERICAN PROFESSOR

No builder today seems to be concerned with the problem of preserving the quiet of the household. The walls of buildings are getting thinner all the time. Ceilings and certain types of new appliances often conduct sounds and noises much better than in the past. Some of our modern buildings are acoustical disasters. Noise pollution has become a major problem in the technological age. Each neighbor knows what the other neighbor does, and neighbors think through a multiplicity of auditory leaks.

THOMAS MERTON
FRENCH-BORN TRAPPIST MONK

The Western tradition — our schools, social institu-
tions, helping professionals, and all their training
support systems, our churches and synagogues —
have very little empathy for solitude. The "togeth-
erness" banner has been strung over every social
institution: families are taught they must do everything together, marriages are built on the foundation
of constant time together (with no options for either
spouse to spend time alone, as if time alone was a
mark of a failing marriage), children are encouraged
to socialize continually, having very little encouragement or practice in spending time alone, corpora-
tions (a set of systems I'm very familiar with) often
are punitive with managers or lower level employees
who want to spend time by themselves (lunches, coffee breaks, dinners out are all times to socialize with
others) — our whole cultural set-up is geared to in-
teractive time. Little wonder that when an individual
starts to grow within himself, starts to develop his
intuitive, transpersonal self, he may find it necessary
to pull back, to learn how to be alone.

MARSHA SINETAR
AMERICAN EDUCATOR

The world would be happier if men had the same capacity to be silent that they have to speak.

SPINOZA, DUTCH PHILOSOPHER

In short, every age has need of "the contemplative
life," and ours is no exception to the rule.... The soul
needs ... a chance for spreading its wings, for looking

beyond itself, beyond the immediate environment, and for quiet inner growth....

JAMES BISSETT PRATT
AMERICAN PHILOSOPHER

We live in a very tense society. We are pulled apart ... and we all need to learn how to pull ourselves together.... I think that at least part of the answer lies in solitude.

HELEN HAYES, AMERICAN ACTRESS

America is the noisiest country that ever existed. One is waked up in the morning not by the singing of the nightingale, but by the steel worker. It is surprising that the sound practical sense of the Americans does not reduce this intolerable noise. All art is based on exclusive and delicate sensibilities, and such continual turmoil must ultimately be destructive to the musical faculties.

OSCAR WILDE, BRITISH NOVELIST

Boredom and ennui, a frantic search for diversion are the common reactions to an hour, or a day of quiet.... We have a compulsion to keep on the move. What keeps the tourist "on the go" is emptiness and incapacity, inability to fill a pause in the day's occupation with anything worth doing: justified fear of leisure time.

WILLIAM MCNAMARA
AMERICAN PHILOSOPHER

Almost all of our woes come from not being capable

of remaining in our rooms.

BLAISE PASCAL
FRENCH MATHEMATICIAN, MORALIST

Nowadays most men live lives of noisy desperation.

JAMES THURBER, AMERICAN HUMORIST

The great omission in American life is solitude . . .
that zone of time and space, free from the outside
pressures, which is the incinerator of the spirit.

MARYA MANNES
AMERICAN SOCIAL CRITIC

Where shall the word be found, where will the word
Resound? Not here, there is not enough silence.

T.S. ELIOT, BRITISH/AMERICAN POET

2

Solitude As Discovery

FINDING THE SELF

If there is a better cure for self-deception than solitude, it has yet to be discovered.

> E. HERMAN, AMERICAN THEOLOGIAN

You turn inward. There's nothing to distract you, so you begin to look at yourself.

> FRANK BIANCO, AMERICAN
> JOURNALIST/PHOTOGRAPHER

I prize the privilege of being alone.

> CARL ROGERS
> AMERICAN PSYCHOLOGIST

You need solitude if you are to fulfill your promises.

> FRANCES STELOFF
> FOUNDER OF GOTHAM BOOK MART

We must, like a painter, take time to stand back from our work, to be still, and thus see what's what. . . . True repose is standing back to survey the activities that fill our days.

WILLIAM MCNAMARA
AMERICAN PHILOSOPHER

In solitude one can achieve a good relationship with
oneself.

MAY SARTON
AMERICAN POET, NOVELIST, ESSAYIST

The goal of a healthy solitude is love: love and accep-
tance of ourselves as we are and where we are, and
love and compassion for others.

DOROTHY PAYNE
AMERICAN PRESBYTERIAN MINISTER

If a woman is to know herself, then periods of solitude should be courted, planned, and embraced.

MARY KAY BLAKELY, AMERICAN HUMORIST

Before you can enjoy your solitude, you have to get
to know yourself — who you are, what you like to
do, what raises your spirits, what gives you a feeling
of accomplishment and exhilaration.

PHYLLIS HOBE, AMERICAN AUTHOR

The most important education you get is your own
— the one you learn in solitude.

ERICA JONG, AMERICAN SOCIAL CRITIC

Only in the oasis of silence can we drink deeply from
our inner cup of wisdom.

SUE PATTON THOELE
AMERICAN PSYCHOTHERAPIST

I love being by myself. And as I grow older, I love
that more than anything else. There are so many
things to think about and work out.

GWENDOLYN BROOKS
POET LAUREATE OF ILLINOIS

In order to get to know yourself, a person needs to be alone with his thoughts now and then.

RICHARD TRIUMPHO, AMERICAN AUTHOR

Avoid the reeking herd,
Shun the polluted flock,
Live like that stoic bird
The eagle of the rock.

ELINOR WYLIE
AMERICAN NATURALIST

And at some time
in your life
trying to be good
may be to stop running
and take time ...
to be quiet
and discover who you are
and where you've been ...

SISTER CORITA KENT
CARMELITE NUN

One lives and endures one's life with others, within matrices, but it is only alone, truly alone that one bursts apart, springs forth.

MARIA ISABEL BARRENO
PORTUGUESE RESEARCHER IN HUMAN RELATIONS

Whatever those unacquainted with it may think, solitude and utter loneliness are far from being devoid of charm. Words cannot convey the almost voluptuous sweetness of the feelings experienced.... Mind and senses develop their sensibility in this contemplative life made up of continual observations and reflections. Does one become a visionary or, rather, is it not that one has been blind until then?

ALEXANDRA DAVID-NEEL
FRENCH-BORN TRAVELER

The insight we gain from solitude has very little to do with the amount of time we spend alone. It has a lot more to do with the quality of time we spend with ourselves.

JAN JOHNSON DRANTELL
AMERICAN COUNSELOR

What a lovely surprise to finally discover how un-lonely being alone can be.

ELLEN BURSTYN, BROADWAY ACTRESS

The choice of solitude is not so much a rejection of community as a recognition that certain experiences and truths are so alien to ordinary consciousness that the individual must withdraw in order to experience them.

CAROL P. CHRIST, AMERICAN PROFESSOR

Nothing strengthens the judgment and quickens the conscience like individual responsibility.... No matter how much women prefer to lean, to be protected and supported, nor how much men desire to have them do so, they must make the voyage of life alone, and for safety in an emergency must know the law of navigation.

ELIZABETH CADY STANTON
AMERICAN POET

Being alone gives us the space to listen again to our inner rhythms, to embrace our inner selves.

PATRICIA HOOLIHAN
AMERICAN WRITER ON SPIRITUAL CONCERNS

We can learn to trust ourselves by inquiring within. To practice doing this, sit quietly, close your eyes, and for a minute focus your attention on your breathing. Gently visualize your inner wisdom as a graceful butterfly. Admire her beauty, and encourage your butterfly to sit on your shoulder and whisper her wisdom in your ear. Be still and listen.

SUE PATTON THOELE
AMERICAN PSYCHOTHERAPIST

There were many times in my life, until I was left alone, that I wished for solitude. I now find that I love solitude. I never had the blessed gift of being alone until the last of my loved ones was wrested from me. Now I can go sometimes for days and days without seeing anyone. I'm not entirely alone, because I listen to the radio and read the newspapers. I love to read. That is my greatest new luxury, having the time to read. And oh, the little things I find to do that make the days, as I say, much too short.

Solitude — walking alone, doing things alone — is the most blessed thing in the world. The mind relaxes and thoughts begin to flow and I think that I am beginning to find myself a little bit.

HELEN HAYES, AMERICAN ACTRESS

There is a need to find and shake our own song, to stretch our limbs and shake them in a dance so wild that nothing can roost there, that stirs the yearning for solitary voyage.

BARBARA LAZEAR ASCHER
AMERICAN LAWYER

Solitude is simply spending time connecting with

ourselves. Solitude means we do it alone, spending time in reflection — perhaps talking to ourselves, writing a journal, meditating. When we practice solitude regularly over a period of time, we develop a deep and abiding connection with our self. We can use that connection to alleviate isolation — from ourselves and others.

JAN JOHNSON DRANTELL
AMERICAN COUNSELOR

Whether living alone is adventure or hardship will depend entirely upon your attitude and your decisions. Become friends with yourself; learn to appreciate who you are and your unique gifts. Be patient with yourself and use your sense of humor to keep things in perspective.

DOROTHY EDGERTON, AMERICAN AUTHOR

Being solitary is being alone well: being alone luxuriously immersed in doings of your own choice, aware of the fullness of your own presence rather than of the absence of others. Because solitude is an achievement. It is your distinctive way of embodying the purposes you have chosen for your life, deciding on these rather than others after deliberately observing and reflecting on your own doings and inclinations, then committing yourself to them for precisely these reasons.

ALICE KOLLER
AMERICAN RELIGIOUS WRITER

In motherhood, more than any other occupation, it is difficult to find time for ourselves. But because of the demands of motherhood, this time of renewing our quiet inner core is very important.... A time for regular exercise, a night out with friends, or taking a class are all ways to affirm who we are as individuals.

PATRICIA HOOLIHAN
AMERICAN WRITER ON SPIRITUAL CONCERNS

Only those who learn how to live with solitude can come to know themselves and life. I go out there and walk and look at the trees and sky. I listen. I sit on a rock or a stump and say to myself, "Who are you, Sandburg? Where have you been, and where are you going?"

CARL SANDBURG, AMERICAN POET

Self-renewal usually begins quietly. The lonely griever becomes a person with a confident solitude.... In contrast to loneliness, which mourns the loss, solitude is positive aloneness, a confident presence of self-suffering.

FREDERIC M. HUDSON
AMERICAN LEADER IN ADULT DEVELOPMENT

In many societies, voluntary isolation from others is considered necessary for the completion of certain phases of personal growth. Adolescent males entering adulthood in certain tribal cultures are expected to wander alone in the forest, mountains, or desert for as long as several months at a time. During this period the solitary wanderer is instructed to communicate with the [divine], compose a song, or experience a magic dream. Those who return without their dream may be sent back into the mountains and told to return when they are successful.

BARBARA POWELL
AMERICAN PSYCHOLOGIST

But women need solitude in order to find again the

true essence of themselves: that firm strand which will be the indispensable center of a whole web of human relationships.

ANNE MORROW LINDBERGH
AMERICAN AUTHOR

Learn to get in touch with silence within yourself and know that everything in this life has a purpose. There are no mistakes, no coincidences; all events are blessings given to us to learn from.

ELISABETH KÜBLER-ROSS
SWISS/AMERICAN PSYCHIATRIST

Alone, but not lonely, I postulate philosophies, explore my soul, and, in the modesty of solitude, expose my love and angers, wishes and disappointments. I examine each, and put it in its place. Alone, I redefine my appreciation of the people with whom I live.

JOAN MILLS, AMERICAN AUTHOR

Living alone, though it may not be the state you ultimately desire for yourself, affords an unparalleled opportunity to know yourself, to be yourself, and to develop yourself as a unique and interesting individual.

PHYLLIS HOBE, AMERICAN AUTHOR

The more faithfully you listen to the voice within you, the better you will hear what is sounding outside. Only he who listens can speak.

DAG HAMMARSKJÖLD
SWEDISH STATESMAN

In these hours and days of dual solitude on the river we hope to discover something quite different, to renew our affection for ourselves and the human kind in general by a temporary, legal separation from the mass. And in what other way is it possible for those not saints?

EDWARD ABBEY
AMERICAN FOREST RANGER

O Solitude, the soul's best friend,
That man acquainted with himself dost make.

CHARLES COTTON, BRITISH POET

Those who aspire to the state of self-discipline should seek the Self in inner solitude through meditation, controlling body and mind, free from expectations and attachment to material possessions.

BHAGAVAD GITA

Solitude is an unending colloquy between you and yourself and such persons as inhabit your memory or are called forth by your imagination. It is painful to have this colloquy interrupted by the voices of real people. "Be still, be still," you want to say to them. "I can't hear what's being said."

JESSAMYN WEST, AMERICAN ESSAYIST

Solitude is the furnace of transformation. Without solitude we remain victims of our society and continue to be entangled in the illusions of the false self.

HENRI J.M. NOUWEN
ROMAN CATHOLIC PRIEST

You think that I am impoverishing myself by withdrawing from men, but in my solitude I have woven for myself a silken web or *chrysalis*, and, nymph-like,

shall ere long burst forth a more perfect creature,
fitted for a higher society.
                              HENRY DAVID THOREAU
                              AMERICAN NATURALIST

It is not difficult to see how dependent simplicity is
upon solitude. Enslavement to the opinions of others
is the source of a great deal of duplicity in modern
society. How often we discover our action to be
prompted, not by the divine Center, but by what
others may say or think. Sadly, we must confess that
our experience is all too frequently characterized by
endless attempts to justify what we do or fail to do.
                              RICHARD J. FOSTER
                              AMERICAN PROFESSOR OF THEOLOGY

By all means use sometimes to be alone.
Salute thyself: see what thy soul
doth wear. . . .

                              GEORGE HERBERT, BRITISH POET

There is nothing either/or about being alone, because it is not a role. It is not a reduced way of life. It
is a possibility for us to participate in a highly creative endeavor: the discovery of our whole selves.
                              PHYLLIS HOBE, AMERICAN AUTHOR

But those who are inwardly alone, whose minds and
hearts are free from the ache of loneliness — they
are real people, for they can discover for themselves
what reality is, they can receive that which is time-
less.
                              J. KRISHNAMURTI, INDIAN PHILOSOPHER

I find there is a quality to being alone that is incredi-
bly precious. Life rushes back into the void, richer,

more vivid, fuller than before. It is as if in parting one did actually lose an arm. And then, like the starfish, one grows it anew; one is whole again, complete and round — more whole, even, than before, when the other people had pieces of one.

ANNE MORROW LINDBERGH
AMERICAN AUTHOR

It is in deep solitude that I find the gentleness with which I can truly love my brothers. The more solitary I am, the more affection I have for them. It is pure affection, and filled with reverence for the solitude of others. Solitude and silence teach me to love my brothers for what they are, not for what they say.

THOMAS MERTON
FRENCH-BORN TRAPPIST MONK

One who has never lived alone has, in fact, missed the opportunity to become a totally independent human being. While this independence can be achieved within a family or communal living experience, I think it is rare. And it is very important that you become a fully independent person before forming a permanent bond with someone else. Otherwise it is too easy, especially for women, to assume the interests and values of a spouse instead of establishing your own.

BARBARA POWELL
AMERICAN PSYCHOLOGIST

I'm the best friend I ever had
I like to be with me.
I like to sit and tell myself
things confidentially.

ANONYMOUS

It is not a bad exercise for a man to sit quiet once in a while and watch the workings of his mind and heart and notice how often he can find himself favoring five or six of the seven deadly sins, and especially the first of those sins, which is named pride.

CARL SANDBURG, AMERICAN POET

That is what is strange — that friends, even passionate love, are not my real life unless there is time alone in which to explore and to discover what is happening or has happened.

MAY SARTON, AMERICAN POET,
NOVELIST, ESSAYIST

The capacity to be alone is a valuable resource when changes of mental attitude are required.

ANTHONY STORR
BRITISH PSYCHIATRIST

Devote six years to your work but in the seventh go into solitude or among strangers so that your friends, by remembering what you were, do not prevent you from being what you have become.

LEO SZILARD, HUNGARIAN PHYSICIST

FINDING GOD

If you wish to grow in your spiritual life, you must not allow yourself to be caught up in the workings of the world; you must find time alone, away from the noise and confusion, away from the allure of power and wealth.

THOMAS À KEMPIS, AUGUSTINIAN MONK

To restore color to our faded personalities and vitality to our languid minds, we must learn to do things, to think things, to *become* someone, alone. If we are to gain from the world of experience and of people what that world has to offer us, we must frequently withdraw from it and find new experiences within ourselves. We need that confidence in ourselves and strength from some Power greater than ourselves which can come to us only from occasional solitude.

MARY ELLEN CHASE
AMERICAN PROFESSOR OF ENGLISH

When we keep a diagnostic eye on our soul, then we can become familiar with the different, often complex stirrings of our inner life and travel with confidence on the paths that lead to the light.

HENRI J.M. NOUWEN
ROMAN CATHOLIC PRIEST

Solitude is when you discover God firsthand. You don't need an intermediary.

BUCKMINSTER FULLER
AMERICAN ARCHITECT, PHILOSOPHER

When you have closed your doors, and darkened your room, remember never to say that you are alone, for you are not alone; God is within, and your genius is within — and what need have they of light to see what you are doing?

EPICTETUS, GREEK PHILOSOPHER

It is an extraordinary fact and an extraordinary piece of evidence for the truth of religion, that long hours spent in silent communication with God who never directly answers is nevertheless manifestly a two-way communication. Such a person is gradually and permanently altered in the depths of his personality in ways which would be inconceivable if there was really "nothing there" at all.

ANONYMOUS

Alone and in silence, I present the whole of my being to God. To say, "Here I am," is to place at his disposal the unique creation he has made. It is to give him this body, with its weaknesses and strengths; this mind, with its confusion and clarity; this heart, with its hardness and pliability. To say, "Here I am," is to offer him the talents he has entrusted to me, using them to their fullest potential. It is to follow him wherever he leads, to stand ready in all situations to be his servant. To ready myself for such a commitment I have to become accustomed to frequent occasions when I stand peacefully and quietly before the Lord — alone and at the same time at one with him. In this aloneness I try gently to quiet the many voices that besiege me in the pressures of daily life in order to listen to his voice in the depths of my being. Outer silence may be sought to foster inner stillness, but it is not necessary. The closer I grow to God, the more I am able to be with him in all circumstances. Whenever he calls I am able to say, "Here I am."

SUSAN ANNETTE MUTO
AMERICAN ACADEMIC, RELIGIOUS EDUCATOR

It is not necessary to go off on a tour of great cathedrals in order to find the Deity. Look within. You have to sit still to do it.

ALBERT SCHWEITZER, GERMAN PHYSICIAN
MISSIONARY, 1952 NOBEL PRIZE WINNER

The highest of all human experiences will be ours when we retire into the Great Empire of Silence and meet with the Eternal Spirit.

ROBERT MERRILL BARTLETT
BRITISH THEOLOGIAN

Jesus can expound nothing until we get through all the noisy questions of the head and are alone with him.

OSWALD CHAMBERS
SCOTTISH EVANGELIST

Whoso, therefore, withdraweth himself from his acquaintances and friends, God will draw near unto him with His holy angels.

THOMAS À KEMPIS, AUGUSTINIAN MONK

Listen to God's speech in his wondrous, terrible, gentle, loving, all-embracing silence.

CATHERINE DE HUECK DOHERTY
RUSSIAN-BORN DIRECTOR GENERAL
LAY APOSTATE OF CATHOLIC ACTION

Settle yourself in solitude, and you will come upon Him in yourself.

ST. TERESA, SPANISH SAINT

There is hardly ever a complete silence in our soul. God is whispering to us wellnigh incessantly. Whenever the sounds of the world die out in the soul, or sink low, then we hear these whisperings of God. He is always whispering to us, only we do not always hear, because of the noise, hurry and distraction which life curses as it rushes on.

FREDERICK W. FABER, BRITISH RECTOR

We must retire from all outward objects, and silence

all desires and wandering imaginations of the mind; that in this profound silence of the whole soul, we may hearken to the ineffable voice of the Divine Teacher. We must listen with an attentive ear; for it is a still small voice.

GUYON FENELON, FRENCH THEOLOGIAN

When we begin to act upon what we feel about life, there is a quiet within. So that we can hear what God has been trying to say to us all along: that He believes in us, that He created us to survive in the world, that He will go with us.

PHYLLIS HOBE, AMERICAN AUTHOR

The silence of prayer is the silence of listening.

ELIZABETH O'CONNOR
AMERICAN FOUNDER, ELDERLY HOUSING PROGRAM

It is only in solitude, when it has broken the thick crust of shame that separates us from one another and separates us all from God, that we have no secrets from God; only in solitude do we raise our hearts to see the Heart of the Universe; only in solitude does the redeeming hymn of supreme confession issue from our soul.

MIGUEL DE UNAMUNO
SPANISH PHILOSOPHER, RECTOR

In all of us there is an inner consciousness that tells of God, an inner voice that speaks to our hearts. It is a voice that speaks to us intimately, personally, in a time of quiet meditation. It is like a lamp unto our feet and a light unto our path. We can reach out into the darkness and figuratively touch the hand of God.

As the Big Book puts it: "Deep down in every man, woman, and child is the fundamental idea of God. We can find the Great Reality deep down within us. And when we find it, it changes our whole attitude toward life."

AA PROGRAM

> Listen, my heart, as only
> saints have listened: until some enormous call
> lifted them off the ground; yet still they knelt,
> those impossible people, undistracted by the
>   sound,
> intent on listening. Not that you could endure
> the voice of God, far from it. But hear what is
>   whispering,
> the endless message forming itself from silence.

RAINER MARIA RILKE, GERMAN POET

Silence is precious, for it is of God. In silence all God's acts are done; in silence alone can his voice be heard and his word spoken.

MOTHER MARY MADELEVA
CARMELITE NUN

In the attitude of silence the soul finds the path in a clearer light, and what is elusive and deceptive resolves itself into crystal clearness. Our life is a long and arduous quest after Truth and the soul requires inward restfulness to attain its full height.

MAHATMA GANDHI
INDIAN SPIRITUAL AND POLITICAL LEADER

We must learn to soundproof the heart against the intruding noises of the public world in order to hear what God has to say.

GORDON MACDONALD, PRESIDENT
INTER-VARSITY CHRISTIAN FELLOWSHIP

Religion is what the individual does with his own solitariness. It runs through three stages, if it evolves to its final satisfaction. It is the transition from God the void to God the enemy, and from God the enemy to God the companion.

Thus religion is solitariness; and if you are never solitary, you are never religious....

ALFRED NORTH WHITEHEAD
BRITISH PHILOSOPHER

We need to find God, and he cannot be found in noise and restlessness. God is the friend of silence. See how nature — trees, flowers, grass — grow in silence; see the stars, the moon and sun, how they move in Silence. . . . The more we receive in silent prayer, the more we can give in our active life. We need silence to be able to touch souls.

MOTHER TERESA
FOUNDER OF SISTERS OF CHARITY, CALCUTTA

Joy [my wife] tells me that once, years ago, she was haunted one morning by a feeling that God wanted something of her, a persistent pressure like the nag of a neglected duty. And till midmorning she kept on wondering what it was. But the moment she stopped worrying, the answer came through as plain as a spoken voice. It was "I don't want you to *do* anything. I want to *give* you something;" and immediately her heart was peace and delight.

C.S. LEWIS
BRITISH CHRISTIAN POLEMICIST

There's a difference between being a solitary person and a lonely person, and believing in God makes the difference. Choosing to be alone with God gives you that connection.

DIANA VREELAND
AMERICAN FASHION DESIGNER

Let us then labour for an inward stillness,
An inward stillness and an inward healing,
That perfect silence where the lips and heart are
  still,
And we no longer entertain our own imperfect
  thought and vain opinions,
But God above speaks in us,
And we wait in singleness of heart,
That we may know His will,
And in the silence of our spirit
That we may do His will,
And do that only . . .

LONGFELLOW, AMERICAN POET

Be still, and know that I am God.

PSALM 46:10

3

Solitude As Inspiration

INWARD PEACE

True silence is the rest of the mind, and it is to the spirit what sleep is to the body, nourishment and refreshment.

WILLIAM PENN, BRITISH QUAKER

We have hints that there is a way of life vastly richer and deeper than all this hurried existence, a life of unhurried serenity and peace and power. If only we could slip over into that center!

THOMAS KELLY, BRITISH EDUCATOR

Serenity springs up when we stop prolonging the winter of our discontent all year round. Great tranquillity of mind and heart can be ours if we are content with the way God has arranged our lives. In the seed of contentment is hidden the rich harvest of serenity.

FLORENCE WEDGE, CANADIAN WRITER

You ask me how I can remain calm and not become upset when those around me are all bustling about. What can I say to you? I did not come into the world to agitate it. Is it not sufficiently agitated already?

ST. FRANÇOIS DE SALES
FRENCH RELIGIOUS MORALIST

A life without a quiet center easily becomes destructive.

HENRI J.M. NOUWEN
ROMAN CATHOLIC PRIEST

For solitude is an attitude, an attitude of gratitude. It is a state of mind, a state of heart, a whole universe unto itself. The early contemplatives in all traditions knew this secret of happiness.

FRANCINE SCHIFF, BRITISH TV PRODUCER

... that perfect tranquillity of life, which is nowhere to be found but in retreat, a faithful friend, and a good library.

APHRA BEHN, BRITISH PLAYWRIGHT

On every mountain height is rest.

GOETHE, GERMAN DRAMATIST

Solitude: a sweet absence of looks.

MILAN KUNDERA, CZECH AUTHOR

There is no species of training that I ever underwent to which I owe more than to the habit of regular periods of inner solitude. Solitary we must be in life's great hours of moral decision; solitary in pain and sorrow; solitary in old age and going forth to death. Fortunate the person who has learned what to do in solitude and brought himself to see what companionship he may discover in it. What fortitude, what content. By a great blessing I had an aptitude for these hours of quiet reflection and grew to love them.... To be alone and still and thoughtful bestowed upon me the richest joy I knew and for this priceless cultivation I shall be thankful always.

WILLIAM SULLIVAN
ROMAN CATHOLIC PRIEST

Don't hurry, don't worry. You're only here for a short visit.

ANONYMOUS

What angel in my own remote childhood taught me when alone to be happy? What gratitude could repay such a boon?

WALTER DE LA MARE, BRITISH POET

Alone, alone! For those who relish it, a word sweeter than muscatel to a wino.

JESSAMYN WEST, AMERICAN ESSAYIST

Genuine tranquility of the heart and perfect peace of mind, the highest blessings on earth after health, are to be found only in solitude and, as a permanent disposition, only in the deepest seclusion.

ARTHUR SCHOPENHAUER
GERMAN PHILOSOPHER

When we are unable to find tranquility within ourselves, it is useless to seek it elsewhere.

ROCHEFOUCAULD, FRENCH PHILOSOPHER

'Tis not in seeking,
'Tis not in endless striving
 Thy quest is found.
 Be still and listen.
 Be still, and drink the silence
 Of all around.
 Not for the crying,
 Not for thy loud beseeching
 Will peace draw near.
 Rest, with palms folded,
 Rest with thine eyelids fallen —
 Lo, peace is here.

EDWARD ROWLAND SILL
AMERICAN POET

[In seclusion] the troubled waters of the mind grow
still and clear, and much that is hidden away and all
that clouds it floats to the surface and can be
skimmed away; and after a time one reaches a state
of peace that is unthought of in the ordinary world.

PATRICK LEIGH FERMOR
BRITISH/IRISH EXPLORER

Thou dost keep him in perfect peace,
whose mind is stayed on thee.

ISAIAH 26.3

O golden Silence, bid our souls be still,
And on the foolish fretting of our care
Lay thy soft touch of healing unaware.

JULIA DORR, AMERICAN POET

I am never less alone than when alone.

CICERO, ROMAN RHETORICIAN

Silence is a friend who will never betray.
                CONFUCIUS, CHINESE TEACHER OF WISDOM

Why do you suppose those moments of solitude
offer us such relief? ...

    Because they give us a chance to simply be our-
selves, to enjoy what and where we are, to savor just
being. Alone with God, we feel no need to perform,
to do.
                                        FRANK BIANCO
                AMERICAN JOURNALIST/PHOTOGRAPHER

It is only in solitude that men and women can come
to know the happiness that is like the delight of children in nothing at all.
            JOHN COWPER POWYS, BRITISH ESSAYIST

Have you ever sat very quietly without any movement? You try it, sit really still, with your back
straight, and observe what your mind is doing. Don't
try to control it, don't say it should not jump from
one thought to another, from one interest to another,
but just be aware of how your mind is jumping.
Don't do anything about it, but watch it as from the
banks of a river you watch the water flow by. In the
flowing river there are so many things — fishes,
leaves, dead animals — but it is always living, moving, and your mind is like that. It is everlastingly
restless, flitting from one thing to another like a butterfly. . . . It is great fun. If you try it as fun, as an
amusing thing, you will find that the mind begins to
settle down without any effort on your part to control it. There is then no censor, no judge, no evalua-
tor; and when the mind is thus very quiet of itself,

spontaneously still, you will discover what it is to be gay. Do you know what gaiety is? It is just to laugh, to take delight in anything or nothing, to know the joy of living, smiling, looking straight into the face of another without any sense of fear.

J. KRISHNAMURTI, INDIAN PHILOSOPHER

Let your mind be quiet, realizing the beauty of the world, and the immense, the boundless treasures that it holds in store. All that you have within you, all that your heart desires, all that your Nature so specially fits you for — that or the counterpart of it waits embedded in the great Whole, for you. It will surely come to you.

EDWARD CARPENTER, AMERICAN POET

Silent in God's presence, you can relax yourself completely. The restfulness of being alone at last, facing reality, may even make you laugh aloud for joy as you open your mind in perfect confidence and summon the whole bustling medley of burdensome thoughts before Him. Let them come, waiting quietly for each, without a shadow of dread. See how they show up in the deep calm of God's presence.

MURIEL LESTER, AMERICAN THEOLOGIAN

I find it wholesome to be alone the greater part of the time. To be in company, even with the best, is soon wearisome and dissipating. I love to be alone. I never found the companion that was so companionable as solitude.

HENRY DAVID THOREAU, AMERICAN NATURALIST

You *can* nurture silence in your noisy heart if you value it, cherish it, and are eager to nourish it.

WAYNE OATES, BAPTIST MINISTER

A certain amount of quiet alone time, whether it is spent meditating, exercising, reading, listening to music, or being creative is, I think, essential for the mental health of most human beings.

BARBARA POWELL, AMERICAN PSYCHOLOGIST

Peace of mind must come in its own time, as the waters settle themselves into clearness as well as quietness; you can no more filter your mind into purity than you can compress it into calmness; you must keep it pure if you will have it pure, and throw no stones into it, if you would have it quiet.

THOMAS RUSKIN, BRITISH ESSAYIST

The most valuable thing we can do for the psyche, occasionally, is to let it rest, wander, live in the changing light of a room, not try to be or do anything whatever.

MAY SARTON, AMERICAN POET,
NOVELIST, ESSAYIST

CREATIVITY

Every kind of creative work demands solitude, and being alone, constructively alone, is a prerequisite for every phase of the creative process.

BARBARA POWELL, AMERICAN PSYCHOLOGIST

Great ideas come into the world as gently as doves. Perhaps, then, if we listen attentively, we shall hear, amid the uproar of empires and nations, a faint flutter of wings, the gentle stirrings of life and hope.

ALBERT CAMUS
FRENCH PHILOSOPHICAL ESSAYIST

I am independent! I can live alone and I love to work. Sometimes it made him [Degas] furious that he could not find a chink in my armor, and there would be months when we just could not see each other, and then something I painted would bring us together again.

MARY CASSATT, FRENCH IMPRESSIONIST

If you are a writer you locate yourself behind a wall of silence and, no matter what you are doing, driving a car or walking or doing housework ... you can still be writing, because you have that space.

JOYCE CAROL OATES, AMERICAN NOVELIST

When the mind is very quiet, completely still, when there is not a movement of thought and therefore no experience, no observer, then that very stillness has its own creative understanding. In that stillness the mind is transformed into something else.

J. KRISHNAMURTI, INDIAN PHILOSOPHER

Every morning you climb several flights of stairs, enter your study, open the French doors, and slide your desk and chair out into the middle of the air. The desk and chair float thirty feet from the ground, between the crowns of maple trees. The furniture is in place; you go back for your thermos of coffee. Then, wincing, you step out again through the French doors and sit down on the chair and look over the desktop. You can see clear to the river from here in winter. You pour yourself a cup of coffee.

Birds fly under your chair. In spring, when the leaves open in the maples' crowns, your view stops in the treetops just beyond the desk; yellow warblers hiss and whisper on the high twigs, and catch flies. Get to work. Your work is to keep cranking the fly-wheel that turns the gears that spin the belt in the engine of belief that keeps you and your desk in midair.

ANNIE DILLARD, AMERICAN NOVELIST

Solitude is good after you're full with what you know. Then you have to be alone and be able to digest it. If you lock yourself up between four walls, and your spirit is empty, and you know only yourself, you will not be able to produce much. But if you are full of the lives of other people, then you can bear solitude, and it's even good for you, because too much of this nourishment is also not good, like everything else. So being alone is good.

ISAAC BASHEVIS SINGER, YIDDISH NOVELIST

The wind is blowing hard . . . I have been painting all day — a painting that should be very good if I can really get it right — another cedar tree — a dead one, against red earth, but the red earth is more difficult — if this one doesn't go I'll try it again. At five I walked — I climbed way up on a pale green hill where I could look all around at the red, yellow, purple formations — miles all around — the color all intensified by the pale gray green I was standing on. It was wonderful.

GEORGIA O'KEEFFE, AMERICAN ARTIST

Back of every blessing of civilization is the scholar and inventor, alone in his room with thought. Out of this solitude comes enrichment of personal life and the discovery of new and glorious conceptions.

ROBERT MERRILL BARTLETT
BRITISH THEOLOGIAN

A public man, though he is necessarily available at many times, must learn to hide. If he is always available, he is not worth enough when he is available.

ELTON TRUEBLOOD, AMERICAN HISTORIAN

The hours which I have spent alone with Mr. Edison have brought me the real big returns of my life: to it I attribute all I have accomplished.

THOMAS EDISON, AMERICAN INVENTOR

Without great solitude no serious work is possible.

PABLO PICASSO, SPANISH PAINTER

I prefer to get up very early in the morning and work. I don't want to speak to anybody or see anybody. Perfect silence. I work until the vein is out.

KATHERINE ANNE PORTER
AMERICAN NOVELIST

What is necessary, after all, is only this: solitude, vast inner solitude. To walk inside yourself and meet no one for hours — that is what you must be able to attain. To be solitary as you were when you were a child, when the grownups walked around, involved with matters that seemed large and important, because they looked so busy and because you didn't understand a thing about what they were doing.

RAINER MARIA RILKE, GERMAN POET

Solitude is as needful to the imagination as society is wholesome for the character.

JAMES RUSSELL LOWELL
AMERICAN JOURNALIST, POET

Silence has wonderful creative power.

ANONYMOUS

I think that the amateur painter may need solitude even more than the professional, for added to the quiet needed for creativity is the desire not to be observed.... I find that I *must* be alone to paint — completely alone. Even if there are people in another part of the house, I don't feel the same freedom. I don't like the feeling that somebody might walk into my space.

BARBARA POWELL, AMERICAN PSYCHOLOGIST

Very few people can write in a crowd. This is a very solitary occupation. I have known people who were more talented than me, who never made it. And the primary reason was always that they couldn't stand to be alone for several hours a day. Any writer worth anything has mastered the art.

The art of solitude.

TOM ROBBINS, AMERICAN NOVELIST

There is nobody else like you. The more you can quiet your own thoughts, fears, doubts, and suspicions, the more will be revealed to you from the higher realms of imagination, intuition, and inspiration.

KENNETH WYDRO, AMERICAN LECTURER

Creative endeavor requires physical and mental space; without privacy, solitude, and time it suffocates. It is not easy to be independent in a crowd and it is impossible to pursue original thought in the scattered remnants of a day or of a lifetime.... Finally, the creative life requires an environment which is free, open, and never so logical and efficient that it cannot be unpredictable.

JUDITH GROCH, AMERICAN PHILOSOPHER

Obviously, if we are to experience insights from our consciousness, we need to be able to give ourselves to solitude.

ROLLO MAY
AMERICAN EXISTENTIALIST PSYCHOLOGIST

Talent is nurtured in solitude; character is formed on the stormy billows of the world.

GOETHE, GERMAN NOVELIST

So that the well-being of the body may not ruin that of the mind, the painter or draughtsman ought to be solitary, especially when he is intent on those reflections and considerations that, by being continually present before his eyes, furnish food to be stored up in memory. If you are alone, you belong entirely to yourself; if you are accompanied by even one companion, you belong only half to yourself, and that much less in proportion to the thoughtlessness of his conduct; and if you have more than one companion, you will fall more deeply into the same plight.

LEONARDO DA VINCI
FLORENTINE PAINTER, SCULPTOR

Oh, to have the luxury of contemplative time! To pour every ounce of energy into creating beautiful things. To train our eye on one — *one* — goal at a time. To give freely without being torn in a thousand directions; to live without apology for what's left undone.

This is true freedom. It's what women yearn for and rarely find. Sparks of inspiration are buried under deadlines and dirty laundry. We're too tired at the end of the day to paint the picture or write the poem that danced through our mid-morning daydreams.

The first step: buy a journal (a notebook will do) and promise to write for ten minutes every day. Do it when you're alone, even if it means locking yourself in the bathroom. Do it religiously.

ELLEN SUE STERN
AMERICAN AUTHOR, LECTURER

What lies before us and what lies beyond us is tiny compared to what lies within us.

HENRY DAVID THOREAU
AMERICAN NATURALIST

Solitude is the nurse of enthusiasm, enthusiasm is the true part of genius.

ISAAC D'ISRAELI, BRITISH ESSAYIST

It seems to me that today, if the artist wishes to be serious — to cut out a little original niche for himself, or at least preserve his own innocence of personality — he must once more sink himself in solitude.

EDGAR DEGAS, FRENCH PAINTER, SCULPTOR

The making of anything really worth making calls for an isolation. Isolation and necessity for intense concentration over a prolonged period of time makes the artist almost antisocial.... They may be isolated, but they're not alone.

WILLIAM SAROYAN, AMERICAN NOVELIST

The things one experiences alone with oneself are very much stronger and purer.

EUGENE DELACROIX, FRENCH ROMANTIC PAINTER

Creative times are quiet, very secretive and lustful.

INGMAR BERGMAN, SWEDISH FILM PRODUCER

Solitude gives birth to the original in us, to beauty unfamiliar and perilous — to poetry.

THOMAS MANN, GERMAN NOVELIST

As regards intellectual work, it remains a fact, indeed, that great decisions in the realms of thought and momentous discoveries and solutions of problems are only possible to an individual, working in solitude.

SIGMUND FREUD, GERMAN PSYCHOANALYST

Silence is the great teacher, and to learn its lessons

you must pay attention to it. There is no substitute for the creative inspiration, knowledge, and stability that comes from knowing how to contact your core of inner silence.

DEEPAK CHOPRA, INDIAN-BORN PHYSICIAN

You cannot be lonely when you are doing a job that can only be done alone.

JANET BONELLIE
CANADIAN INTERIOR DESIGNER

There is a remarkable picture called Contemplation. It shows a forest in winter and on a roadway through the forest, in absolute solitude, stands a peasant in torn kaftan and bark shoes. He stands, as it were, lost in thought. Yet he is not thinking: he is "contemplating." If anyone touched him he would start and look bewildered.

In time he would come to himself immediately; but if he were asked what he had been thinking about, he would remember nothing. Yet probably he has hidden within himself, the impression which dominated him during the period of contemplation. Those impressions are dear to him and he probably hoards them imperceptibly, and even unconsciously. How and why, of course, he does not know. He may suddenly, after hoarding impressions for many years, abandon everything and go off to Jerusalem on a pilgrimage. Or he may suddenly set fire to his native village. Or he may do both.

FYODOR DOSTOEVSKY, RUSSIAN NOVELIST

The actual process of writing ... demands complete, noiseless privacy, without even music; a baby howling two blocks away will drive me nuts.

WILLIAM STYRON, AMERICAN NOVELIST

If I were to describe solitude I would say there are an enormous amount of stimulating things, mostly paper, letters, and books which are all saying: "Pay attention to me." Very often they are much more interesting than people because people talk back. Things can't.

MARY HEMINGWAY, WRITER
LAST WIFE OF THE LATE ERNEST HEMINGWAY

I can't be anything for [my readers] unless I write, and I can only write with a lot of peace — a very quiet daily life, with very few things and a very few close friends.

PETER HOEG, DANISH NOVELIST

When we are in the act of writing we are alone and on our own, in a kind of absolute state of Do Not Disturb.

EUDORA WELTY
AMERICAN NOVELIST, SHORT FICTION WRITER

4

Solitude and the Natural World

The best remedy for those who are afraid, lonely, or unhappy is to go outside, somewhere where they can be quite alone with the heavens, nature, and God.

ANNE FRANK, GERMAN DIARIST

The feeling of wonder, of awe, of fearful joy, of ecstatic and rapturous contemplation, in the presence of the mystery behind what we call Nature.

JOHN COWPER POWYS, BRITISH ESSAYIST

But for the time being, around my place at least, the air is untroubled, and I become aware for the first time today of the immense silence in which I am lost. Not a silence so much as a great stillness — for there are a few sounds: the creak of some bird in a juniper tree, an eddy of wind which passes and fades like a sign, the ticking of the watch on my wrist —

slight noises which break the sensation of absolute
silence but at the same time exaggerate my sense of
the surrounding, overwhelming peace. A suspension
of time, a continuous present. If I look at the small
device strapped to my wrist the numbers, even the
sweeping second hand, seem meaningless, almost
ridiculous. No travelers, no campers, no wanderers
have come to this part of the desert today and for a
few moments I feel and realize that I am very much
alone.... I wait. Now the night flows back, the
mighty stillness embraces and includes me; I can see
the stars again, and the world of starlight. I am
twenty miles or more from the nearest fellow
human, but instead of loneliness I feel loveliness.
Loveliness and a quiet exultation.

EDWARD ABBEY
AMERICAN FOREST RANGER

Being female and domestic, even when young, I
wanted to be alone in a place of my own. I was no
baby Byron or Shelley. I had no wish for the solitude
of sea or mountaintop, though I liked these well
enough, too. But such outdoor solitude didn't need,
when I was young, to be stolen. The beaches of La-
guna and Newport, of Balboa and La Jolla were still
empty. The hills of Yorba Linda were inhabited only
by other lovers of solitude: coyotes, rattlesnakes,
buzzards. They wanted to be alone as much as I.

JESSAMYN WEST, AMERICAN ESSAYIST

Our adventures in beauty are always closely bound
up with our silent moods. A mountain vista, the

unbounded sea, or a sunset hush and still the feeble efforts we make to define art.

ROBERT MERRILL BARTLETT
BRITISH THEOLOGIAN

In childhood and boyhood this ecstasy overtook me when I was happy out of doors. Was I five or six? Certainly not seven. It was a morning in early summer. A silver haze shimmered and trembled over the lime trees. The air was laden with their fragrance. The temperature was like a caress. I remember — I need not recall — that I climbed up a tree stump and felt suddenly immersed in Itness. I did not call it by that name. I had no need for words. It and I were one.

BERNARD BERENSON
LITHUANIAN ART HISTORIAN

I have come back to my solitude, my joy, and I am sure these radiant skies have much to do with it.

MAY SARTON, AMERICAN POET,
NOVELIST, ESSAYIST

I loafe and invite my soul,
I lean and loafe at my ease observing
A spear of summer grass.

WALT WHITMAN, AMERICAN POET

People talk about the silence of nature, but of course there is no such thing. What they mean is that *our* voices are still, *our* noises absent.

SUE HALPERN, AMERICAN PROFESSOR

The attraction of berry picking is that it offers time

for quiet contemplation. If the mosquitos and deer flies aren't biting, and if the heat isn't intolerably humid, a person can enjoy an hour or two of busy solitude....

While the fingers are busy plucking berries, the mind is free to wander. Your thoughts go skipping, seemingly aimlessly, contemplating the briars, the plump berries, the song of a bird, the satisfactions and frustrations that happened to you last week. Such reflection puts perspective on one's life, makes you realize where you have been, gives awareness of the forces that shape you into the kind of person you are, makes you better able to deal with where you are going.

RICHARD TRIUMPHO, AMERICAN AUTHOR

At 11:00 A.M. the launch puts me ashore and I walk up on the ridge overlooking the sea. Even Nature in her harsher aspects in the tropics soothes and heals. I stand and loiter long on the breezy ridge and look north upon the great blue crescent of the sea. I have but one thought, and am glad to be alone with it on the hills.

JOHN BURROUGHS, AMERICAN NATURALIST

I was sitting at my desk and looking out the bay window at some swaying trees and those bright autumn leaves that have not yet fallen to the ground. It is quiet, and I am alone. At this moment I choose to allow the quiet to surround and penetrate me. I can feel the concerns, and plans, and details of an ordinary, busy day recede for a time. I can feel myself quieting down....

OLIVER MORGAN
AMERICAN LECTURER, AUTHOR

I surround myself with silence. The silence is within me, permeates my house, reaches beyond the surfaces of the outer walls and into the bordering woods. It is one silence, continuous from within me outward in all directions: above, beneath, forward, rearward, sideward. In the silence I listen, I watch, I sense, I attend. I observe. I require this silence. I search it out. The finely drawn treble song of a white-throated sparrow is part of it. Invasions of it by the noise of engines are torments to me.

This is my solitude.

ALICE KOLLER, AMERICAN RELIGIOUS WRITER

The night comes softly, beyond the power line and the blacktop, where the long-abandoned wagon road fades amid the new growth. It does not crowd the lingering day. There is a time of passage as the bright light of the summer day, cool green and intensely blue, slowly yields to the deep, virgin darkness. Quietly, the darkness grows in the forest, seeping into the clearing and penetrating the soul, all-healing, all-reconciling, renewing the world for a new day. Were there no darkness to restore the soul, humans would quickly burn out their finite store of dreams.

ERAZIM KOHAK
CZECH-BORN PROFESSOR OF PHILOSOPHY

As the night advanced it changed its spirit and garments to ampler stateliness. I was almost conscious

of a definite presence, Nature silently near. The great
constellation of the Water-Serpent stretched its coils
over more than half the heavens. The Swan with out-
spread wings was flying down the Milky Way. The
northern Crown, the Eagle, Lyra, all three in their
places. From the whole dome shot down points of
light, rapport with me, through the clear blue-black.

EDGAR COLLARD, CANADIAN JOURNALIST

The environing world of a forest clearing is calm and
unjarring, living its own familiar life, so unlike the
threatening, unpredictable environment of the arti-
fact world.

ERAZIM KOHAK
CZECH-BORN PROFESSOR OF PHILOSOPHY

I lived once in the American desert. The solitude
opens up. It becomes an enormous surrounding
comfort.

VIVIAN GORNICK, AMERICAN PROFESSOR

Standing quietly in the water, feeling the sand shift-
ing away under my toes ... I lay back in the floating
position that left my face to the sky, and shoved off.
The sky wheeled over me. For an instant, as I bobbed
into the main channel, I had the sensation of sliding
down the vast tilted face of the continent. It was then
that I felt the cold needles of the alpine springs at my
fingertips, and the warmth of the Gulf pulling me
southward. Moving with me, leaving its taste upon
my mouth and spouting under me in dancing
springs of sand, was the immense body of the continent itself, flowing like the river was flowing, grain
by grain, mountain by mountain, down to the sea. I

was streaming over ancient sea beds thrust aloft
where giant reptiles had once sported; I was wearing
down the face of time and trundling cloud-wreathed
ranges into oblivion.... I was streaming alive
through the hot and working ferment of the sun, or
oozing secretively through shady thickets. I was
water....

LOREN EISELEY, AMERICAN ENVIRONMENTALIST

In solitude we are in the presence of mere matter
(even the sky, the stars, the moon, trees in blossom),
things of less value (perhaps) than the human spirit.
Its value lies in the greater possibility of attention. If
we could be attentive to the same degree in the presence of a human being.

SIMONE WEIL, FRENCH MYSTIC

With the passage of days in this godly isolation
[desert], my heart grew calm. It seemed to fill with
answers. I did not ask questions any more; I was certain. Everything — where we come from, where we
are going, what our purpose is on earth — struck me
as extremely sure and simple in this God-trodden
isolation. Little by little my blood took on the godly
rhythm. Matins, Divine Liturgy, vespers, psalm-
odies, the sun rising in the morning and setting in
the evening, the constellations suspended like chan-
deliers each night over the monastery: all came and
went, came and went in obedience to eternal laws,
and drew the blood of man into the same placid
rhythm. I saw the world as a tree, a gigantic poplar,
and myself as a green leaf clinging to a branch with

my slender stalk. When God's wind blew, I hopped
and danced, together with the entire tree.

NIKOS KAZANTZAKIS, GREEK POET, NOVELIST

We stand, every day and every night, in the very
presence of a power so incomparable as to make the
senses reel. And yet, happily, this power — the intel-
ligence behind all the marvels of the summer sky —
is a benevolent one. The man who pays attention
will hear, deep within his soul, a quiet and friendly
voice saying: "This, and so much more also, is yours
to share."

VERNON R. HARRIS
AMERICAN RELIGIOUS WRITER

The voice of the sea is seductive; never ceasing,
whispering, clamoring, murmuring, inviting the
soul to wander for a spell in abysses of solitude; to
lose itself in mazes of inward contemplation.

The voice of the sea speaks to the soul. The
touch of the sea is sensuous, enfolding the body in
its soft, close embrace.... She turned her face sea-
ward to gather in an impression of space and solitude, which the vast expanse of water, meeting and
melting with the moonlit sky, conveyed to her excit-
ed fancy. As she swam she seemed to be reaching out
for the unlimited in which to lose herself.

KATE CHOPIN, AMERICAN NOVELIST

Nature seemed to me full of wonders, and I wanted
to steep myself in them. Every stone, every plant,
every single thing seemed alive and indescribably
marvelous. I immersed myself in nature, crawled, as

it were, into the very essence of nature and away from the whole human world.

CARL GUSTAV JUNG, SWISS PSYCHIATRIST

I, a city dweller, have a summer place on a cedar-crested bluff overlooking a lovely bay down by the sea. The salt breezes off the mighty ocean sweep cares away; the soft sunlight falling on the grass teaches me the quiet repose of earth; the unhurried sounds of the natural world, so different in quality from strident city noises, quiet me as a mother soothes her troubled child; and at night when the stars come out, blossoming one by one in the infinite meadows of heaven, and a hush falls over land and sea, I can hear the friendly voice of Mother Nature, which is the voice of God, saying: "My child, this is life. Take time to live it."

NORMAN VINCENT PEALE
AMERICAN THEOLOGIAN

There is a pleasure in the pathless woods,
There is rapture on the lonely shore,
There is society where none intrudes,
By the deep Sea, and music in its roar;
I love not man less, but Nature more.

LORD BYRON, BRITISH POET

I also sometimes go down into that valley, which is the most secret part of my wilderness (*desert*), and which until now was not known to anyone.... If I pause ever so little there, it seems to me that I return to my first innocence. My desires, my fears and my hopes cease all of a sudden; all the movements of my soul abate and I have no passions whatsoever, or if I have any, I govern them like tamed beasts.

HONORÉ DE BALZAC, FRENCH NOVELIST

Is there another country in the world in which the silence is so perfect? Here in the land of the Eskimos there is no wind in the trees, for there are no leaves. No birds sing. There is no noise of flowing water. No frightened animals flee away in the dark. There is no stone to become loose under human feet and fall down a river bank, for all these stones are walled in by the frost and buried under the snow. And yet this world is far from dead: it is only that the beings which dwell in this solitude are noiseless and invisible.

This stillness which had been so solitary, which had calmed me and done good to my worn-out nerves, gradually began to weigh on me like a lead weight. The flame of life within us withdrew further and further into a secret hiding place, and our heartbeats became ever slower. The day would come when we should have to shake ourselves to keep our heartbeats going. We had sunk deep into this silence, we were paralyzed by it, we were on the bottom of a well from which we could pull ourselves out only with inconceivable difficulty.

GONTRAN DE PONCINS
FRENCH ARCTIC EXPLORER

The pure beauty of the Canadian water, the somber but august grandeur of the vast forest that hemmed us in on every side and shut us out from the rest of the world, soon cast a magic spell upon our spirits, and we began to feel charmed with the freedom and solitude around us.

SUSANNA MOODIE
CANADIAN POET, AUTOBIOGRAPHER

I walk without flinching through the burning cathedral of the summer. My bank of wild grass is majestic and full of music. It is a fire that solitude presses against my lips.

VIOLETTE LEDUC, FRENCH NOVELIST

[The desert]: clean air to breathe (after the spring sandstorms); stillness, solitude and space; an unobstructed view every day and every night of sun, sky, stars, clouds, mountains, moon, cliffrock and canyons; a sense of time enough to let thought and feeling range from here to the end of the world and back; the discovery of something intimate — though impossible to name — in the remote.

EDWARD ABBEY, AMERICAN FOREST RANGER

I very frequently used to retire into a solitary place, on the banks of Hudson's River, at some distance from the city, for contemplation on divine things and secret converse with God, and had many sweet hours there.

JONATHAN EDWARDS, AMERICAN PASTOR

We readily attribute some extra virtue to those persons who voluntarily embrace solitude, who live alone in the country or in the woods or in the mountains and find life sweet. We know they cannot live without converse, without society of some sort, and we credit them with the power of invoking it from themselves, or else of finding more companionship with dumb things than ordinary mortals. In any case they give evidence of resources which all do not possess.

JOHN BURROUGHS, AMERICAN NATURALIST

Among the hills, when you sit in the cool shade of the white poplars, sharing the peace and serenity of distant fields and meadows — then let your heart say in silence, "God rests in reason."

KAHLIL GIBRAN
LEBANESE-AMERICAN PAINTER, POET

It all adds up to one thing: peace, silence, solitude. The world and its noise are out of sight and far away. Forest and field, sun and wind and sky, earth and water, all speak the same silent language.

THOMAS MERTON
FRENCH-BORN TRAPPIST MONK

I got up at sunrise and was happy; I walked, and was happy; I roamed the forests and hills, I wandered in the valleys, I read, I did nothing, I worked in the garden, I picked the fruit, I helped in the house, and happiness followed me everywhere — happiness which could not be referred to any definite object, but dwelt entirely within myself and which never left me a single instant.

ROUSSEAU, SWISS-BORN ESSAYIST

Sometimes, on a summer morning, having taken my accustomed bath, I sat in my sunny doorway from sunrise till noon, rapt in a revery, amidst the pines and hickories and sumachs, in undisturbed solitude and stillness, while the birds sang around or flitted noiseless through the house, until by the sun falling in at my west window, or the noise of some traveller's wagon on the distant highway, I was reminded of the lapse of time.

HENRY DAVID THOREAU
AMERICAN NATURALIST

If you have ever sat on a mountain top and surveyed the country below, you must realize that what you saw was even more beautiful because of the awesome silence which surrounded you. Art galleries maintain a quiet because curators realize that a painting viewed in the midst of noise is less beautiful than when it is contemplated in the midst of silence. One really cannot appreciate the great art treasures housed in museums on days when noisy crowds gather around every object to be viewed.... The beauty of art will show itself in greater force in the midst of silence. Not only does silence enhance the beauty of art, but adds to the experience its own sublime beauty.

KARL PRUTER, AMERICAN BISHOP

Of all the gifts of a place by the sea, perhaps the greatest is the gift of solitude.

ANONYMOUS

I come to my solitary woodland walk as the homesick go home.

HENRY DAVID THOREAU
AMERICAN NATURALIST

The ideal surrounding for the study of oneself is some untouched bit of the outdoors, which, in spite of man's exploitation of nature, still offers relatively secluded spots for meditation.

PHILIP WYLIE, AMERICAN NOVELIST, ESSAYIST

Lie down and listen to the crabgrass grow,
The faucet leak, and learn to leave them so.
Feel how the breezes play about your hair
And sunlight settles on your breathing skin.
What else can matter but the drifting glance
On Dragonfly or sudden shadow there
Of swans aloft and the whiffle of their wings
On air to other ponds? Nothing but this:
To see, to wonder, to receive, to feel
What lies in the circle of your singleness.
Think idly of a woman or a verse
Of bees or vapor trails or why the birds
Are still at noon. Yourself, be still —
There is no living when you're nagging time
And stunting every second with your will.
You work for this: to be the sovereign
Of what you slave to have — not
Slave.

MARYA MANNES
AMERICAN JOURNALIST, SOCIAL CRITIC

I identify with nature and all of life very deeply, so I
can just lose myself to the surroundings. Every little
insect, and every quiver of a leaf matters to me.

ROSALYN TURECK
AMERICAN CONCERT ARTIST

When I begin to sit with the dawn in solitude, I
begin to really live. It makes me treasure every single moment of life.

GLORIA VANDERBILT
AMERICAN ACTRESS, FASHION DESIGNER

Any inner exploration can be helped or hindered by the outer conditions.... When I'm in the mountain retreat, nothing is happening outside, it's all happening inside.

JAMES GEORGE, U.S. SENATOR

Being able to sail well, to love it, to understand it, to do it safely and thoughtfully, to be able to go out on the sea when you want to find congeniality with nature, to feel the tide, the wind, the channel. All that is a complex of inputs which is most relaxing. It is my solitude.

BRITTON CHANCE
BRITISH BIOCHEMIST, BIOPHYSICIAN

5

Other Places of Solitude

AT HOME

I like a great library next to my study; but for the study itself give me a small snug place, almost entirely walled with books. There should be only one window in it, looking upon trees.

LEIGH HUNT, BRITISH POET, ESSAYIST

It is the place of renewal and of safety, where for a little while there will be no harm or attack and, while every sense is nourished, the soul rests.

MAY SARTON, AMERICAN POET,
NOVELIST, ESSAYIST

I feel most alone in an empty house. A house was made for people, and their absence makes the rooms more empty than any forest can ever be. Or even any desert. In a way you can never be alone outside. Outside is too populated. (Is the moon "outside"?)

Inside, emptied of its inhabitants, is a shell whose original tenant has passed away. Completely. You are alone and an intruder in a house not your own, and this doubles the aloneness. Perhaps burglars are solitaries, and theft is only a sideline with them. The real high comes not from the money or the tape recorders, but from being alone where they ought not to be.

JESSAMYN WEST, AMERICAN ESSAYIST

It is a place for what is important to you — reading, study, work, prayer, quiet withdrawal — and it should be used for that purpose alone.

ERNEST BOYER, JR., AMERICAN CHAPLAIN

Louisa had almost the enthusiasm of an artist over the mere order and cleanliness of her solitary home.

MARY E. WILKINS FREEMAN
AMERICAN NOVELIST

Here in this house of wind and willow boughs
Quietness is my constantly only guest.

AUDREY ALEXANDRA BROWN
CANADIAN POET, ESSAYIST

There should be at least a room or some corner where no one will find you and disturb you or notice you. You should be free to untether yourself from the world and set yourself free, loosing all the fine strings and strands of tension that bind you, by sight, by sound, by thought, to the pressure of other men. Once you have found a place, be content with it, and do not be disturbed if a good reason takes you

out of it. Love it, and return to it as soon as you can.
THOMAS MERTON
FRENCH-BORN TRAPPIST MONK

> Oh! For a book, and a cozy nook
> And Oh! for a quiet hour,
> When care and strife and worry of life,
> Have lost their dreaded power....
>
> ANONYMOUS

I have at last got the little room I have wanted so long, and am very happy about it. It does me good to be alone.
LOUISA MAY ALCOTT, AMERICAN NOVELIST

> Days of work! the only days I really lived!
> O much cherished solitude!
> God be praised, I have returned
> To this old study!
> Poor little nook, walls so many times deserted,
> Dusty armchairs, faithful lamp,
> O my palace, my little universe....
>
> ALFRED DE MUSSET, FRENCH ROMANTIC POET

I have a house where I go.
When there's too many people.
I have a house where I go
Where no one can be;
I have a house where I go,
Where nobody ever says "NO"
Where no one says anything — so
There is no one but me.
A.A. MILNE, BRITISH
PLAYWRIGHT, POET, CHILDREN'S AUTHOR

Tub, piano box, a room of my own, here a little house of my own — what have I been seeking? Womb remembered, tomb anticipated? The edifice isn't the answer. It's what the edifice, tub or trailer provides: solitude. It is the universe, its inward flow unendangered by human distraction. There is a pattern of light and shadow on my floor, columns of light, pillars of dark, in which I can live as they shift and change. There is a whisper of wind around the lifted front shutter. There is the smell of deep, running water.

JESSAMYN WEST, AMERICAN ESSAYIST

I have often thought that the best mode of life for me would be to sit in the innermost room of a spacious locked cellar with my writing things and a lamp. Food would be brought and always put down far away from my room, outside the cellar's outermost door. The walk to my food, in my dressing gown, through the vaulted cellars, would be my only exercise. I would then return to my table, eat slowly and with deliberation, then start writing again at once. And how I would write! From what depths I would drag it up!

FRANZ KAFKA
GERMAN NOVELIST OF CZECH ORIGIN

You will find that deep place of silence right in your room, your garden, or even your bathtub.

ELISABETH KÜBLER-ROSS
SWISS/AMERICAN PSYCHIATRIST

"And when you pray, you must not be like the hypocrites; for they love to stand and pray in the synagogues and at the street corners, that they may be

seen by men. Truly, I say to you, they have their reward. But when you pray, go into your room and shut
the door and pray to your Father who is in secret; and
your Father who sees in secret will reward you."

MATTHEW 6:5-6

We must reserve a back shop all our own, entirely
free, in which to establish our real liberty and our
principal retreat and solitude. Here our ordinary
conversation must be between us and ourselves, and
so private that no outside association or communication can find a place; here we must talk and laugh as
if without wife, without children, without possessions, without retinue and servants, so that, when
the time comes to lose them, it will be nothing new
to us to do without them.... Let us not fear that in
this solitude we shall stagnate in tedious idleness:
"In solitude be to thyself a throng."

MONTAIGNE, FRENCH ESSAYIST

I have three chairs in my house: one for solitude, two
for friendship, and three for society.

HENRY DAVID THOREAU, AMERICAN NATURALIST

A feeling that was unfamiliar but very delicious
came over her. She walked all through the house,
from one room to another, as if inspecting it for the
first time. She tried the various chairs and lounges,
as if she had never sat and reclined upon them before.... The flowers were like new acquaintances.

KATE CHOPIN, AMERICAN NOVELIST

I wander through unpeopled rooms, listening to the
large, soft silence, giving myself over to being all

alone. It is like a return to having a very private place in which to know oneself, and grow.... No one knows if I am up and functioning, or if I am shamelessly snoring at noon. I can type at midnight, and nobody comes to glare and mutter. No one bangs on the bathroom door when I linger long in the tub, turning the hot water on and off with my toes and sloshing deliciously. No critic comments upon my working at crewel through the supper hour and dining much later by the flickering light of the late show.

JOAN MILLS, AMERICAN AUTHOR

IN HOUSES OF WORSHIP

I like the silent church before the service begins, better than any preaching.

RALPH WALDO EMERSON
AMERICAN PASTOR, ESSAYIST

It is the great strength of the Society of Friends that their Meeting for Worship ... consists of a handful of men and women, often less than a score, rarely exceeding fifty or a hundred, who sit together for about an hour, for the most part in silence, in an ordinary room or hall. The silence is broken only if someone in the Meeting feels "called to the ministry." When this happens, the one so stirred normally speaks, for some few minutes perhaps, often less, of something that has come to him out of the silence. He may be followed by one or two others, equally brief, typically taking up the same thread and continuing it.

When it is successful (which, needless to say, is not always) the Quaker Meeting for Worship is indubitably a method by which the deep centre is experienced and the experience transmitted. How this comes about is at present a matter of surmise rather than knowledge. Partly, no doubt, it is due to the concerted seeking in silence. Since there is little to distract attention, the libido is free for inward exploration, for the discovery of the Kingdom.

P. W. MARTIN
AMERICAN PHILOSOPHER

[The Cistercian churches] filled anyone who entered them with peace and restfulness and disposed the soul for contemplation in an atmosphere of simplicity and poverty.

THOMAS MERTON
FRENCH-BORN TRAPPIST MONK

After a hymn and the Rosary, you disappear into the utter solitude of the evening meditation. You kneel in your stall with all your Sisters around you and your Lord on His throne before you. And you are completely alone in the company you love best on earth.

MOTHER MARY FRANCIS
ROMAN CATHOLIC NUN

I love old-Meeting-houses, — how my heart
Goes out to those dear silent homes of prayer
With all their quietude and rustic charm,
Their loved associations from old days,

Their tranquil and pathetic solitude,
Their hallowed memories!
I love old Meeting-houses; — how remote
From all the world's loud tumult do they
    seem! —
Islands of blissful peace to lull tired souls
Tossed on the seas of daily circumstance
And seeking friendly haven after storm;
To shelter and to shield.

JOHN RUSSELL HAYES
AMERICAN TRAVEL WRITER

Our life is organized above all for prayer.... Every-thing in our life tends to protect us from the turmoil of the world and of our passions, to guarantee us solitude of the spirit, the heart and the will, in order that our monasteries may be sanctuaries of silence filled with the fragrance of prayer, where nothing is heard but the voice of the soul praising God and of God replying to the soul.

DON VITAL LEHODEY, FRENCH TRAPPIST MONK

Dost thou love silence deep as that "before the winds were made"? Go not out into the wilderness, descend not into the profundities of the earth; shut not up thy casements; nor pour wax into the little cells of thy ears, with little-faith'd self-mistrusting Ulysses. — Retire with me into a Quakers' Meeting.

CHARLES LAMB, BRITISH POET, ESSAYIST

Under the guidance of divine grace, in the school of charity, in the silence of the cloister, we are to be gradually initiated into a deep and experimental

knowledge of the truth — first, as it is found in ourselves, then as it is found in other men and, finally,
as it is in itself.

THOMAS MERTON
FRENCH-BORN TRAPPIST MONK

AMONG OTHERS

The soul that has made a habit of interior solitude
can withdraw, even in the presence of those it cares
for most, into its secret communion with the Inani-
mate; and instead of this withdrawal weakening its
feeling for this other one, or for these others, it in-
creases it.

JOHN COWPER POWYS, BRITISH ESSAYIST

Years of close familiarity rendered silence conge-
nial. . . .

COLETTE, FRENCH NOVELIST

Solitude can become your most meaningful companion and it can assist you in being a more giving person in your spiritual partnerships. Rather than
regarding your partner's need for time alone as a
threat, see it as a time of renewal that you celebrate.
Make every effort to help each other have that space.
Treat that space as sacred.

WAYNE W. DYER, AMERICAN PROFESSOR
CONSULTANT TO HOSPITALS

Sometimes we are just two people together but
alone, quietly recharging.

LOUISE LAGUE, AMERICAN AUTHOR

Solitude is fragile and too rare. When two people make a pact that there won't be any intrusions from outside, real serenity is possible.... Solitude for two provides us with regular blocks of time when we know we have each other to look forward to, the freedom to be ourselves to do whatever we wish and unhurried time to spend together.

ALEXANDRA STODDARD
AMERICAN INTERIOR DESIGNER

There is a hush in a home on the morning after death, a silence that would be violated by too many words.

EMILY DICKINSON, AMERICAN POET

Silent discourse prevails where people are deeply involved with one another. The collective awareness is developed to such an extent that it becomes a religious experience, and it can be neither uttered in sound nor communicated in words.

JOHN HOSTETLER, AMERICAN THEOLOGIAN

The love that consists in this:
that two solitudes protect
and border
and greet each other.

RAINER MARIA RILKE, GERMAN POET

Among friends one has the privilege of saying nothing; the civility consists in the assumption that one's silence will be civilly understood. I can imagine a small gathering of friends who say nothing all evening: they recoil from saying anything that the others don't want to hear; and their silence would be the subtlest courtesy.

ALLEN TATE, AMERICAN POET, CRITIC

Not everyone knows how to be alone with others, how to share solitude. We have to help each other to understand how to be in our solitude, so that we can relate to each other without grabbing on to each other. We can be interdependent but not dependent. Loneliness is rejected dependency. Solitude is shared interdependency.

DAVID SPANGLER, SCOTTISH PHILOSOPHER

It is easy in the world to live after the world's opinion; it is easy in solitude to live after our own; but the great man is he who in the midst of the crowd keeps with perfect sweetness the independence of solitude.

RALPH WALDO EMERSON
AMERICAN PASTOR, ESSAYIST

WITHIN THE HUMAN HEART

To love solitude and to seek it does not mean constantly travelling from one geographical possibility to another. A man becomes a solitary at the moment when, no matter what may be his external surroundings, he is suddenly aware of his own inalienable solitude and sees that he will never be anything but solitary. From that moment, solitude is not potential — it is actual.

THOMAS MERTON
FRENCH-BORN TRAPPIST MONK

The human heart has hidden treasures,
In secret kept, in silence sealed.

CHARLOTTE BRONTË, BRITISH NOVELIST

If you cannot go into the desert, of you is required the solitude of mind and of heart. You will be safe there, if there you do not think, if there you do not love, if there you do not act as they think, as they love, as they act in the world.

ST. JEROME, ROMAN HERMIT
TRANSLATOR OF SCRIPTURES

The holiest of all holidays are those
Kept by ourselves in silence and apart;
The secret anniversaries of the heart.

LONGFELLOW, AMERICAN POET

I think to have a place is important. I speak of it even before the question of time because, making the time ... we have to have some place to spend it. Moreover, a constituted place stands there beckoning to us, reminding us to make the time.... The important thing is that there is this place which, when one goes there, even if the going is no more than turning one's chair around, one has a sense of having gone apart.... Not to be neglected in this apartness is that precious cell in the heart. There is deep within us a place apart.... Come apart and rest awhile. In its deep, cool darkness, sometimes illumined by a light not of our making, a moment can be a refreshing step into eternity, a coming home to the solitude of God.

M. BASIL PENNINGTON
ROMAN CATHOLIC PRIEST

Silence does not depend upon your being alone. Whether you are in a streetcar, or in a church, teaching a class, or working as a typist, you can still be immersed in the Silence of God. If you are immersed in this silence, the little things you do — scrub floors, wash carrots, work on a farm or in an office — will be a thunder that spans the divide between sun and moon.

CATHERINE DE HUECK DOHERTY
RUSSIAN-BORN DIRECTOR GENERAL,
LAY APOSTATE OF CATHOLIC ACTION

All the nobler instincts of our race are born in solitude and suckled by silence. This solitude need be no faraway wilderness in Nature; this silence need be no Himalayan Peak. You stop for a second as you cross your city square and glance at the Belt of Orion. You lie awake for a while as you rest in your bed and listen to the storm; and behold! from a few simple elements belonging to that mystery which you have been brought up to call "Matter," there suddenly comes over you this reversion, this conversion, this transmutation of spirit.

JOHN COWPER POWYS, BRITISH ESSAYIST

A man thinking or working is always alone, let him be where he will.

HENRY DAVID THOREAU, AMERICAN NATURALIST

And that was what now she often felt the need of — to think; well, not even to think. To be silent; to be alone. All the being and the doing, expansive, glittering, vocal, evaporated; and one shrunk, with a sense of solemnity, to being oneself, a wedge-shaped core of darkness, something invisible to others. Although she continued to knit, and sat upright, it was thus that she felt herself; and this self having shed its attachments was free for the strangest adventures. When life sank down for a moment, the range of experience seemed limitless.... This core of darkness could go anywhere, for no one saw it. They could not stop it, she thought, exulting. There was freedom, there was peace, there was, most welcome of all, a summoning together, a resting on a platform of stability.

VIRGINIA WOOLF, BRITISH NOVELIST

An inner garden is often the most powerful solace we can find.

SUE PATTON THOELE
AMERICAN PSYCHOTHERAPIST

The inside room was a very private place. She could be in the middle of a house full of people and still feel like she was locked up by herself.

CARSON MCCULLERS
AMERICAN SHORT FICTION WRITER, NOVELIST

It is not needful always to be in church to be with God. We make a chapel of our heart, to which we can from time to time withdraw to have gentle, humble, loving communion with Him.

BROTHER LAWRENCE, LAY BROTHER
AMONG CARMELITES AT PARIS

Inside myself is a place where I live all alone, and that's where you renew your springs that never dry up.

PEARL BUCK
CHINESE-AMERICAN AUTHOR, MISSIONARY

Every morning, lean thine arms awhile
Upon the window sill of heaven,
And gaze upon the Lord....
Then, with that vision in thy heart,
Turn strong to meet the day.

ANONYMOUS

Nothing is at last sacred but the integrity of your
own mind.... Trust thyself: every heart vibrates to
that iron strong.

RALPH WALDO EMERSON
AMERICAN PASTOR, ESSAYIST

Interior silence, she repeated silently. That would be
her Waterloo. How without brain surgery could you
quell the rabble of memories. Even as she asked herself the question, she heard her psychology professor saying quite clearly across a space of years, "No
one, not even a saint, can say an *Ave* straight
through without some association creeping in; this is
a known thing."

KATHRYN HULME, AMERICAN AUTOBIOGRAPHER

When I need solitude, I turn off the phone and fax
and sit until my breath comes slow and gentle, and I
am able to enter into the sanctuary that always
awaits me at the center of my being.

SAM KEEN, AMERICAN SPIRITUAL TEACHER

Within you there is a stillness and a sanctuary to
which you can retreat at anytime and be yourself.

HERMANN HESSE, GERMAN NOVELIST, POET

6

The Power of Silence

What a strange power there is in silence! How many resolutions are formed, how many sublime conquests effected, during that pause when lips are closed, and the soul secretly feels the eye of her Maker upon her! They are the strong ones who know how to keep silence when it is a pain and grief unto them, and who give time to their own souls to wax strong against temptation.

RALPH WALDO EMERSON
AMERICAN PASTOR, ESSAYIST

... a time to keep silence, and a time to speak.

ECCLESIASTES 3:7

The apron of silence is with me. Silence is a gift. Be silent.

CLARA SANDBURG
MOTHER OF THE AMERICAN POET

The victories of speech have been many, but the victories of silence have been more. The man of silence is the man of power.

CARL SANDBURG, AMERICAN POET

In almost every field of human endeavor in which speech plays an important role, so likewise does silence. And the more meaningful the one, the more expressive the other. The drama, formal religion, public meetings — all exemplify the enhancement of speech by the contrast with silence. So does education, as when the skilled teacher makes a deliberate pause to allow main points to sink in, or new ideas to be assembled. Not so different all this, from the use of shadow by the artist to bring out lights and highlights.

ALICE BORCHARD GREENE
AMERICAN PHILOSOPHER

I stop and taste my words before I let them pass my teeth.

ANONYMOUS

Silence speaks, the contemplatives say. But really, I think, silence sorts. An ordering instinct sends people into the hush where the voice can be heard.... Silence, that inspired dealer, takes the day's deck, the life, all in a crazy heap, lays it out, and plays its flawless hand of solitaire, every card in place. Scoops them up, and does it all again.

PATRICIA HAMPL, AMERICAN PROFESSOR

There is something greater and purer than what the

mouth utters. Silence illuminates our souls, whispers to our hearts, and brings them together.

KAHLIL GIBRAN
LEBANESE-AMERICAN PAINTER, POET

He that would live in peace and ease must not speak all he knows nor judge all he sees.

BENJAMIN FRANKLIN
AMERICAN STATESMAN, AUTHOR

Silence is the unbearable repartee.

ALEXANDER THEROUX
AMERICAN ESSAYIST, PLAYWRIGHT

This was the best thing she had known, to walk down streets interminably ... her head cool, watchful, alert, waiting for the coming of the visitor, silence.

DORIS LESSING, RHODESIAN NOVELIST

Those who are silent, self-effacing and attentive become the recipients of confidences.

THORNTON WILDER
AMERICAN NOVELIST, PLAYWRIGHT

One of the greatest sounds of them all — and to me it is a sound — is utter, complete silence.

ANDRE KOSTELANETZ
RUSSIAN-BORN CONDUCTOR

To communicate through silence is a link between the thoughts of man.

MARCEL MARCEAU, FRENCH PANTOMIMIST

To live a contemplative life is to be open enough to

see, free enough to hear, real enough to respond. It is a life, and so has its own rhythms of darkness, of dying-rising. Simply enough, it is a life of grateful receptivity, of wordless awe, of silent simplicity.

SISTER MARIE BEHA, ROMAN CATHOLIC NUN

Silence is for me a fount of healing which makes my life worth living. Talking is often a torment for me, and I need many days of silence to recover from the futility of words.

CARL GUSTAV JUNG, SWISS PSYCHIATRIST

In music we gain a sense of rhythm through the absence of sound. A similar process occurs in communication between two people.

SHELDON ROTH
AMERICAN PSYCHOTHERAPIST

Certain experiences may be transmitted by language, others — more profound — by silence; and then there are those that cannot be transmitted, not even by silence.

ELIE WIESEL
RUMANIAN HOLOCAUST SURVIVOR

He who speaks does not know, he who knows does not speak.

ANONYMOUS

If we want to understand the essence of silence, we need only think of those moments in life when the silence of love becomes a reality for us. We are referring to the delicate mutual understanding of those in love or of friends, which can perfectly express itself in mere being together, jointly contemplating.

LADISLAUS BOROS, GERMAN-BORN AUTHOR

Deliberately to choose to be silent at times, to watch and weigh our words when we speak, would accomplish more for many than the pious practices they so much enjoy.
BEDE FROST, AMERICAN THEOLOGIAN

There are times when silence is the most sacred of responses.
EUGENE KENNEDY, AMERICAN PHILOSOPHER

Silence must be comprehended as not solely the absence of sound. It is the natural environment for serenity and contemplation. Life without silence is life without privacy. The difference between sanity and madness is the quality of our thoughts. Silence is on the side of sanity.
NORMAN COUSINS
AMERICAN PHILOSOPHER, ESSAYIST

The deepest sympathy that we can express is that which we give in quiet understanding. Exhausting the trite expressions used for the solace of the unfortunate we say: "My friend, we are one in this sorrow. I take upon myself the burden that you bear. We shall no longer struggle to explain or talk away this tragedy. We shall fall back to the peace of God's presence and be still!"
ROBERT MERRILL BARTLETT
BRITISH THEOLOGIAN

If people would only hold their tongues on unpleasant topics, how the things themselves would improve.
E.F. BENSON, BRITISH NOVELIST

Silence is one great art of conversation.
WILLIAM HAZLITT, BRITISH ESSAYIST

Next to entertaining or impressive talk, a thorough-going silence manages to intrigue most people.

FLORENCE HURST HARRIMAN
AMERICAN SOCIALITE, POLITICAL ACTIVIST

Speak not but what may benefit others or yourself. Avoid trifling conversation.... None preaches better than the ant, and she says nothing.

BENJAMIN FRANKLIN
AMERICAN STATESMAN, AUTHOR

I have learned silence from the talkative, toleration from the intolerant, and kindness from the unkind; yet strange, I am ungrateful to those teachers.

KAHLIL GIBRAN
LEBANESE-AMERICAN PAINTER, POET

Silence gives consent.

OLIVER GOLDSMITH, BRITISH NOVELIST

That man's silence is wonderful to listen to.

THOMAS HARDY, BRITISH NOVELIST

There is a silence that matches our best possibilities when we have learned to listen to others. We can master the art of being quiet in order to be able to hear clearly what others are saying.... We need to cut off the garbled static of our own preoccupations to give to people who want our quiet attention.

EUGENE KENNEDY, AMERICAN PHILOSOPHER

Blessed is the man who, having nothing to say, abstains from giving us wordy evidence of the fact.

GEORGE ELIOT, BRITISH NOVELIST

Better to remain silent and be thought a fool than to

speak out and remove all doubt.

ABRAHAM LINCOLN
SIXTEENTH AMERICAN PRESIDENT

Silence is a great peacemaker.

LONGFELLOW, AMERICAN POET

Blessed are they who have nothing to say, and who cannot be persuaded to say it.

JAMES RUSSELL LOWELL
AMERICAN PROFESSOR, POET

The deepest feeling always shows itself in silence; not in silence, but restraint.

MARIANNE MOORE, AMERICAN POET

Be silent and safe — silence never betrays you.

JOHN BOYLE O'REILLY, IRISH-BORN NOVELIST

Even a fool who keeps silent is considered wise....

PROVERBS 17:28

Silence alone can bring two hearts closer together.

KARL PRUTER, AMERICAN BISHOP

He knew the precise psychological moment when to say nothing.

OSCAR WILDE, BRITISH NOVELIST

Talking is a loss of power.

FREDERICK W. FABER, BRITISH RECTOR

Nothing in a statesman's arsenal is more effective than a weapon that he might not even know he has: silence.

RICHARD M. NIXON
THIRTY-SEVENTH AMERICAN PRESIDENT

Practice silence and you will acquire silent knowledge. In this silent knowledge is a computing system that is far more precise and far more accurate and far more powerful than anything that is contained in the boundaries of rational thought.

DEEPAK CHOPRA, INDIAN-BORN PHYSICIAN

A silent tongue makes sweet music for the soul.

ANONYMOUS

There is a certain dignity in silence.

NANCY REAGAN
WIFE OF THE FORTIETH AMERICAN PRESIDENT

An elaborately patient silence can be very provoking!

C.S. LEWIS, BRITISH CHRISTIAN POLEMICIST

Silence means you are under complete control of all your emotional reactions, which are conquered in silence. Everything that happens in our bodies happens in complete silence. And when you start hearing from it, then you know something is wrong! The principle of healing is to invoke silence — going into the silence.

MOTHER SERENA
LEADER IN THE ROSICRUCIAN SOCIETY

"Better say nothing at all. Language is worth a thousand pounds a word!"

LEWIS CARROLL, BRITISH HUMORIST

The more words, the more reflection
The less you understand the Way,
Cut off words, cut off reflection
And you penetrate everywhere.

BUDDHIST VERSE

What I love most of all is the *silence*. It's the silence that works. Silence is marvelous . . . Whew! It's gorgeous. No sounds . . . nobody . . . no touching . . . I walk through the door, and there it is waiting for me in the room. I have instant silence!

JOAN FONTAINE, AMERICAN FILM ACTRESS

Silence is unceasing eloquence. It is the best language.

RAMANA MAHARSHI
SPIRITUAL TEACHER, INDIA

About the Editor

DALE SALWAK is professor of English at Southern California's Citrus College. He was educated at Purdue University and then the University of Southern California under a National Defense Education Act competitive fellowship program. In 1985 he was awarded a National Endowment for the Humanities grant. In 1987 Purdue University awarded him its Distinguished Alumnus Award. He is widely published, including fifteen other books on various contemporary literary figures.

Bibliographic Index

The information in this index allows the reader to locate the contributions of authors within the text and to explore their writing.

The Classic Wisdom Collection

If you would like a catalog of our fine
books and cassettes, contact:

New World Library
58 Paul Drive
San Rafael, California 94903
(415) 472-2100
FAX (415) 472-6131

Or call toll-free: (800) 227-3900